I0439418

FRESH BREEZES BLOW

A journey through the trauma of childhood rape

By

Patricia Joyce Parker Miller

December 31, 2013

DEDICATION

For the journeys of my parents and all my family.

To all my friends and mentors: my late husband, Ronald Miller, Mary Leslie, the late Dr. Brugh Joy, Ceil Levisky, Suzi Hamilton, Joan Liljedahl, the late Phyllis "Petey" Stark Salman, Dr. Janet Schreiber, Dianne Barnes, the Children's Grief Center in Albuquerque, NM., Marty Glenn, Desiree Woodland; the doctor who encouraged me to write my story, Dr. Kothandopany Shalini; a bone-marrow thankfulness to my compassionate companion, Jan Boyer, and last, but not least, my poetry writing compadres, Geri Saunders and Paul Baca, and my wonderful editor, Erica Grong.

Thank you for our journeys together.

Patricia Joyce Parker Miller aka "Trish" – December 31 2013

If you are reading this now, it's because you have been raped as a child. This is my journey navigating through the shoals of loneliness, fear, rage, shame, grief, sadness, betrayal and depression, after rapes.

To heal required reflection on my early childhood: what it was like before the rapes; what I believe made me so vulnerable Growing up in a little railroad town in southern New Mexico - Rincon - about 35 miles north of Las Cruces, my first memories were at four or five years old, 1940-1943. Mom and Dad worked for the Atchison, Topeka and Santa Fe Railroad (ATSF), so my brother, David, and I did what we pleased, and pretty much on our own. I remember being angry, maybe because we were alone so much. Neither my Mother nor Father showed much emotion, which was not uncommon in those days. Neither of them had mothers or fathers that hugged them, told them they were loved or had words to explain things. What was missing was being touched, held and comforting words - a basic need for children - that sense of unconditional love. It was mostly 'don't do that' or 'you mustn't feel that way' from Mom. Dad scared me to death trying to teach us about rattlesnakes. It was the time when kids were seen and not heard, the mantra of the late 40's and 50's.

One of our jobs, as responsible human beings, is to find the meaning of our lives, to ask the questions. Why am I here? What is mine to do? Not that I can unravel the Mystery, but unwinding my own personal drama, and hopefully helping someone else out of their own mind-boggling journey of the primal violation of childhood innocence of rape which results in fear, guilt, shame and self-hate is one way.

I have come to believe that all of us are loved by the Creator of our universe; all of us worthy, all of us came from One Source. There are many names for God, the Creator, the Divine, the One, Allah, Jehovah, or Vishnu, just as I believe there are many paths.

+++++++++++++++++++++

The memoir contains both prose and poetry, and is graphic in content. The following poem, "A Sense of Love", was written in 2012 at 76 years old. It was one of those 'aha' moments, thinking about Rincon, the Episcopal Church, the school, the railroad, and the neighbors. We all knew each other. What was it about that safe, little town that I remembered with such loving, fond memories? The poem emerged.

A SENSE OF LOVE

Something indefinable surrounded me,
seeped into me, unknowing, a sense of sweetness,
safety, warmth, loving, and caring.

A small white church
with a tall steeple stood at the top of the hill,
south of town.   Sunday school was large sand
tables at the back of the small sanctuary.
The stained-glass windows let the
sun's rays make prisms

of rainbows on the floor. I could almost
see the fairies dancing with joy.
I moved the small figures as the
stories were read to us.
I loved Jesus on the donkey.

It was WWII. I was 5 years old. Mom played
the pump organ. We sang all the military hymns,
all five verses. I especially liked The Marine Corps hymn.
My favorite, though, was "Eternal Father, Strong to Save".
I felt safe.

The preacher was
Preacher Hunter Lewis, a kindly man.
I never knew what he said. He was just sweet.
Later I learned that he hitch-hiked all over
Southern New Mexico, had had
St. Vitus' Dance as a kid. His sister taught
him to knit. He knitted caps for

all the babies he baptized. He knit while he was
waiting for a ride, in a car, on horseback,
in a buggy, or while he rested beside the road.
He cared for everyone.

It was a place separate from no words,
or missing being held and cuddled,
being scared of snakes, scared of doing
or saying something wrong.
Fear was not there.
It was learning a sense of oneness.

It was my first knowing and sensing
the Love that surrounds and infuses
us with what we call the presence of God.

I started this story with a poem about my sense of Love;

because I am convinced we have one or several of those times

in our lives. That the Holy Spirit dwells within us all is

undeniable. Whether we call that Spirit, the Holy Spirit or

the indwelling Christ Spirit or God within is not important.

What is important is that we know that we are God's

creations. Knowing we are Loved, without conditions, I

believe is the first instinctual need of humans. My knowing

did not consciously manifest until I was in my 70's. I had to dig into my inner sanctum to find that sense of Love.   It is what this story is about, finding my path, finding the Light within. The journey is individual and different for each.

The beliefs that I learned as a child have had to be examined: Had I committed terrible 'sins'? Was I going to 'hell'? Were the rapes my fault? Was I a 'fallen woman' that nobody wanted because I had had 'sex'? Was I loved by God? How could I love myself?   Could I be forgiven? Did I need to forgive myself? Did I need to forgive others? What about guilt, shame, and anger that I carried with me? What do I do about those and all the other intense feelings? Who am I, anyway? The beliefs I carried – I was sinful; I was going to hell; God didn't love me; I wasn't lovable; everything was my fault; no one would want me because I had had sex outside of marriage; I was a fallen woman --are now called 'imbedded beliefs'. Some is the DNA we inherited from the cell structures of our parents. Other beliefs were those of the culture at the time, and what our parents had learned from their time of growing up in the Victorian Era, and on and on. The search is to discover me, and change the DNA and the inherited wounded cells. And, fortunately, the cultural values have changed. Still, the journey is life-long and not easy.

I pray that relating my journey will help you.

+++++++++++++++++++++++++++++++

The following happened to me as a ten-year old child, accounts of primal rape.

Jim and Vel were our next-door neighbors. They had two children, Frances, who was married to Lonnie with whom she had had three young boys, and Jimmy, my best friend. Jimmie was two years younger than me, and we always played together. The summer of 1945, Frances and her husband, Lonnie, moved in with Vel and Jim. In retrospect, I wonder if Lonnie had lost his job, so they had to move in with her parents. Lonnie, a really good looking man was liked by all the neighborhood kids. We, including Lonnie, played hide-and- seek, kick the can, tag, and whatever games we could think up. Lonnie was fun and friendly, like a kid, he was one of us. I was really pleased, too, that I seemed to be the person he liked the most. One night he suggested that he take us all out to Storrie Lake. We could play hide-and-seek there. It would be more fun. We piled in his car for our great adventure. When we got there, we hid. Lonnie was appointed to find us. He found me first. He asked me to sit in the car with him. I had been taught to obey my parents, do what I was told by adults, never question or say anything, to be seen and not heard. So, I got in the car with him. He began talking to me, telling how much he liked me. He asked me to sit closer. He put his arm around me. I felt so special and safe. He began fondling the place between my legs. I liked him, and it felt good. My head was buzzing. Pretty soon, he unbuttoned his trousers, and a huge, throbbing 'thing' – that's what we kids called it- stuck straight up. He said, "Put your mouth on it!" I did as I was told. It was sickening. I thought I was going to throw up. That's all I remember about that episode. A few days later, Mom and Dad were at work. I was home by myself. There was a knock on the door. It was Lonnie. I let him in. He led me to my bedroom, pushed me down on the bed, pulled my pants down and stuck his big 'thing' in me. He pushed back and forth for awhile, and then pulled it out. A bunch of sticky stuff got all over the quilt on my bed. About the time he was leaving, David came home, either I told him or he realized what had happened. He told Mom. When she and Dad came home from work, Mom called our family doctor. He came to our house, took Mom and me to his office for an examination. He said, "I don't think she's pregnant." After we got home, I was in the backyard playing. I peeked around the corner to see Dad, our neighbor and Lonnie sitting on the front lawn. I think Dad may have threatened Lonnie if he ever came near me again. He never did. I had such mixed feelings. I was filled with guilt and shame. I had lost what I thought was a friend.

That horrific event in my childhood was never mentioned again – no words, no nothing. It was my fault, I was the one responsible. I don't remember much of anything after Mom took me to the doctor. I have fuzzy memories of knowing it took 9 months to have a baby. I was submerged in fear for 9 months. The only other thing I remember is when David, said his name, Lonnie, at the dinner table. The food I had eaten started coming up. I knew I had to swallow the food and the emotions, if I wanted dessert. I forced myself to swallow the food and everything else.. I believed with my whole being that I was going to hell. The guilt was like layer upon layer of mud that encased my heart and soul.

Long after the first rape, there were two other rapes that scarred my childhood. I can't remember which one was first.

I was ten years old in the 4rd grade. I made friends with Dottie. Her family was rich. They had two ranches and horses, and a house in town. Making sure that I was her most important friend, I curried favor. I wanted to ride horses. Eventually, she invited me to her ranch. She taught me how to saddle a horse, how to get on and how to ride. My favorite horse was a brown, chestnut named 'Stardust'. I loved riding. It was heavenly. Dottie's parents were never around. I think she was lonely, too. She had a brother, Billy, who was 4 years older than Dottie.

One afternoon at her house, we were playing in the back bedroom. Billy came down the hallway into the room. He pushed me down on the lower bunk bed, pulled down my panties, unzipped his levis and pulled out his big 'thing' and rammed it into me. He was like a big bull humping a cow. It hurt. I didn't cry or scream; only sissies cried. Dottie sat across the room and watched. Now, I think he raped her, too. I didn't know what to do.

We were at the ranch when Billy caught me and raped me again. He pinned me down in the barn. I was surprised and horrified. There were other feelings, too, more guilt, more shame, pleasure, distaste, hatred of self and pure animal lust.

In the 5th or 6th grade, I went with Mom to visit our former neighbors in Rincon. I had known them all my life. Our Dads both worked for the Santa Fe Railroad. David and

I and Bobby, their son, played together as kids. One time Bobby was walking the picket fence. He fell and was held upside down by the cuff of his pants by a sharp picket. I thought it was funny and laughed. I found out later that he had broken his leg. This particular day, Bobby said, "Let's go play in the basement." We no sooner got down the stairs till Bobby pushed me down on a sleeping bag, pulled down his pants and stuck his 'thing' in me. He proceeded to ram it in and out as he breathed his halitosis breath on me. We went back upstairs and acted like nothing had happened. I hated him for a long time. Maybe he raped me as payback for laughing when he broke his leg. Who knows?

++++++++++++++++

Because these violent incidents were not addressed immediately, one of my jobs has been to work, stop and go, through the issues associated with rape most of my life. Like all of us, many of the choices I made after these shattering experiences were the result of buried trauma.

Some of the issues I've already written about, but I want you to know that the learning process is not sequential. It comes in fit and starts, sometimes zig-zags. Once written down does not mean that the particular issue goes away, it just means I am more aware of it, and know how to deal with it more effectively.

A huge issue for children who have been raped is the sense of boundaries or loss of innocence. I was in my late 40's, married, with two children in the 1980's when psychologists began talking about 'boundaries' and what happens when our self boundaries are ruptured by the violation of rape.

Years later, in talking to my counselor about boundaries, I asked her how our self boundaries get re-established. She described it as an inside out process. The following poem describes how I felt as I've reestablished my

own inner self boundaries.

BOUNDARIES

What are they?
In the physical world,
a fence, a border of flowers,
walls, measured property,
a boundary determined by law,
like a state boundary.
In the inner world, the womb.

The shock and trauma of birth
disrupts safety and warmth.
that initial boundary replaced
by another invisible boundary
of innocence which gets
nurtured, hopefully, by
the nursing body of mother,
the cradling of family.

If and when the negative energies of
fear, rage, helplessness and hate
shatter the boundaries of innocence,
their giant axes drive wedges
in the heart, and contaminate the soul.

Once those elements are embedded
in heart and soul,
they coalesce into

a slow burning I.E.D.
Shrapnels of fear, rage, and hate
explode into anyone and everyone
who triggers the burning fuse.

Each negative element
has to be identified and
traced to the source
to be neutralized.

Required is precision and skill.
filled with agony, despair,
confusion and depression,
determination and patience,
a monumental task.

Slowly the cesspool of
trapped, negative energy
begins to release
and the soul responds.

When the heart is able to
hear the clarion call of Love,
a compassionate companion,
the stillness within is
there, waiting, helping
to halt the conditioned patterns
of response.
The resident tutor helps
plant seeds of growth,
new beliefs, new thoughts,

new ways to respond,
rooted in Love.

The boundaries of Self
reinflate from within
with Love, knowing,
safety and forgiveness.

Boundaries become secure.
the sacredness of Self
is home.

Establishing boundaries is not necessarily the first step

in healing from the trauma of rape. It's a new way of

knowing how to protect myself. It, too, is an ongoing process,

as I think it is for many of us.

++++++++++

At eleven years old, my perception of God was an old

white-bearded man in the sky who watched, punished or

threatened with going to 'hell' if I did anything wrong. The

belief filled with me unrelenting guilt and shame; added to

those two, after the rapes, was the feeling helplessness. The

helplessness manifested in me   as thoughts of 'nobody cares', 'it doesn't matter' or 'what's the use'. Some researchers now say that shame and guilt are direct consequences that arise in the body from the primal fear emanating from rape experience. I believe, too, that shame and guilt are those 'embedded beliefs' that have origins in the way the culture, parents and the church presented their interpretations of God. God was a god to be feared, and yet one that had to be worshipped.

+++++++++++++++++++++++

Looking at my life experiences, many were grounding and helpful, some not so much. In the 7th grade, I attended a youth church camp where I 'accepted Jesus Christ as my Lord and Savior', which, in retrospect, added more guilt and shame - feeling superior and 'saved'. Was it helpful? At one level of the psyche, perhaps I was more aware of God, At the time, though, it was only words. It deepened my ability to bury emotions. I had learned well from my parents. I could say certain words, but words did not heal the subconscious learned responses.

Learning to play the trombone in the 3rd grade was helpful and healing, a serendipity circumstance. Champ Tyrone, the teacher, came from Indiana, sort of like the movie, "The Music Man". He put his hand on my diaphragm and taught me how to breathe, never, ever touching me in an inappropriate way. I trusted and loved him. Using my breath to make music enabled me to expel some of the accumulating grief.

High school was filled with boyfriends, and achievement. Joining the Order of Rainbow for Girls, a closed group, at my Mother's request, was a helpful structure or boundary. I was a leader with Mom working beside me. It was ritualistic and safe. Years later, I realized that Mom helped, not so much with words, but with persistence,

presence, and probably a lot of prayer.

After high school and being somewhat arrogant, I

unknowingly went to a religious fundamental college. A

poem best describes my experience.

<u>College</u>
<u>1954-1958</u>

Going to a small Christian school,
I'll be safe, I thought.
Located at 79th and Vermont in Los Angeles,
blue buildings and a music scholarship appealed.
Rigid theology ruled, chapel
every morning, no piano, no organ,
accapella voices, and surprisingly
good harmony. The preacher
professors proclaimed, "You're wrong".
An arrogant, self-absorbed English
professor blacked-out ribald parts
of Shakespeare and Chaucer. He
missed the best parts.

The dean of the college was
compassionate, a superb teacher, and
profound thinker. A few teachers
were superb, and I learned.

Sophomore year brought,
catastrophic restructuring, school
in the red, moderate teachers fled,
The dean fired. The powers that be
brought in more rigidity.
more holier-than-thou professors.

Two years of stability, such as it was,
gone. Most students in a
state of shock, new faces, new teachers,
new dean. Inter-Varsity, an
ecumenical Christian group emerged.
Met Ron, a blinded veteran.
Read for him, fell in love,
felt safe. He had money, and
a car,

Last year of college,
married, in an apartment,
happy and safe, or so I thought.
1958 and graduation.

When I married, Ron, I thought I was safe. He had

money, a disability pension from the U.S. Government as a

Blinded Veteran. I believed we were in love. We made a

deep connection, but mostly it was lust. I knew that I was

hiding; no other man would marry a 'fallen woman'. The

poem relates my experience   of our marriage.

TWO WOUNDED SOULS

Marriage was a snake-pit
of betrayal. We had yawning
caverns of repression.
Two wounded souls
came together,
one blind, one sighted,
Both lived in
glass houses of beliefs
filled with shame, guilt,
anger and self-loathing.
His anger scared me.
I said mean things.
He withdrew.
I withdrew.
It was the 50's.
Divorce was not in the cards.

What to do?
Have a child. move.
new job. Have another child.
Trapped.
His infidelity began.
He got sick, nearly died.
We moved south, Ph.D. program,
five years of relentless work,
nose to the grindstone.
more infidelity, my heart broken, again
and again.

Steady as she goes.
What to do?
Tried meditation. My heart-chakra opened.

Fear gripped him. He shut down.
Tried Marriage Encounter,
inner work too much for him. so
new job. He moved north by himself.
Me with two teenagers. more
infidelity. I moved north.
Four years of stability.
Then, power and glory called.
We moved east.
Eight years of hard work for him, stress
scary Metro rides, conflict with
co-workers, and more infidelity.
He moved out.
Diane, our daughter, became ill, a
deadly disease, in the
hospital for a month.
It was 1995.

She almost died. gut-wrenching
sadness and grief.
I asked him to come back.
"You don't need me,"
He said, and hung up.

Work, friends, depression,
counseling, and three years later,
divorce.

Within a year later after the trauma of the divorce and Diane being so desperately ill, I had three surgeries: left kidney removed (renal carcinoma), back surgery a year later. and a week after 9/11, removal of my gallbladder. I didn't know that I had stored and pushed down the entire early trauma from the rapes. I had learned the lessons well – 'don't cry', 'keep your chin up', 'don't wear your feelings on your sleeve', etc. etc. The divorce and Diane being so ill, catapulted me into finally beginning to realize that I needed help. My friend said, "I think you're depressed." I got mad. Then, I realized she was right. I saw a counselor in Maryland for 2-3 years before I retired and moved to Albuquerque, New Mexico in 2004.

++++++++++++++++++++++++++++++++++++++

Loving self, learning to forgive and learning to listen to the body responses, are huge issues for those who have been raped. The vignette that follows details how I first learned to forgive.

We were attending a Presbyterian Church in Huntington Beach, California. The minister was, Don Roberts, an enlightened soul, who preached Love and forgiveness. In a meditation seminar, the leader told us to find a safe place and invite someone I could totally trust. The Sangre de Christo Mountains, north of Las Vegas, where my folks had a cabin was the safest place. I invited Jesus. The minister said, tell the person what happened. He said, "Can you forgive this person?" In my case, it was Lonnie. I said, "Absolutely not." We emerged from meditation. He said, "So, you can't forgive. It's not important. The important thing is that you are honest with yourself and with God; the Spirit works in your heart always." A year later, I attended the same seminar. I forgave. It was absolute honesty that enabled me to forgive him, thirty years later.

One of the best things I did was attend seminars given by Dr. Brugh Joy, an Internist at the University of Southern California Medical Center turned spiritual teacher who interpreted dreams, taught opening the 'heart shakra' and heart-centered meditation To my amazement I learned that I had 'white-washed' away the horrific events of rape. One way to express the idea of 'white-washing' was to realize that I had worn many masks. A poem best expresses it.

MASKS

What is a mask anyway?
Is it a covering,
a hiding, a protective device?
Do we all wear masks?
or is there a time
when we don't need one?

I know there is no mask
for raw grief,
tear-stained cheeks,
no cover-up; grief connects us.
to bone-marrow sadness
we share, but seldom show.

Behind my masks
lies a lifelong pattern of hiding,
from myself and God.
Loneliness, sadness
fear, guilt, shame.
feeling unloved, self-hate,
are the roots.
White-wash everything,
make a joke,
make others laugh.
Here are some of my masks.

The Rebel mask
Trauma, fight, flight or freeze,
consciousness said - rebel, be angry,
live with no answers, no words.
I don't trust you.
Don't tell me what to do.
My first Halloween
Mom made me
a Devil Suit.
Someone pulled off my devil's tail.
I went into a rage.
I was five years old.

The Religion mask.
Hope for relief from
negative thoughts and beliefs.
I'm forgiven and frozen, learning
arrogance, self-righteousness, and
superiority.
I'm better than you

I'm okay.
You're not.

The Achievement mask.
Look at me.
Look at my accomplishments.
Look how good I am.
I'm somebody.

The Martyr mask.
I'll fix you, because
I can't fix me.
I'll sacrifice myself.
Thirty-eight years of marriage
is enough.

The Mother mask.
The authority figure,
The one who knows.
The one in charge.

Microscopic viewing reveals
The pattern of hiding and revelation,
a constant recommitment,
a work in progress.

+++++++++++++++

A year after my Mother died in 2005, I began to work on my grief and trauma, I attended Southwestern College in Santa Fe specializing in trauma and grief counseling, learning that trauma and carried grief had gotten 'stuck' in my body. The illnesses were the way grief manifested in me. A most invaluable lesson was a type of therapy called "Somatic Experiencing", developed by Dr. Peter Levine. Jan Boyer, MA, LPCC, SEP, from Santa Fe introduced this type of therapy to the class.

In 2008, putting our wonderful dog, Bosco, 'to sleep' after a five-month bout with bone cancer and my frantic efforts in trying to 'fix' him, was the catalyst that finally broke open my frozen places.

In his book, <u>Waking the Tiger</u>, Dr. Levine introduced 'Somatic Experiencing', as an original and scientific approach to the healing of trauma, such as rape: an approach

31

based on understanding the communication between our thoughts, our body sensations, and our physiology, teaching that the body can heal the psychological scars of trauma. They can be transformed if we listen to communications from our body. When we experience trauma, our human instinctual physiological response is to fight, take flight or freeze or become immobilized. Most of us who have experienced rape as children freeze, resulting in the energy or adrenaline being stuck in the body. Anther way of describing the 'frozen' or immobilized experience is to imagine driving a car with one foot pressing the gas pedal to the floor with the other foot on the brake. The car, like the body, gets stuck or frozen in place.

Somatic Experiencing uses the "felt sense" – the instinctual response of the body ("not a mental experience, but a physical one", Levine, p. 67) - rather than emotions to gradually and gently work through the terror, rage and helplessness of rape. Too much focus on thoughts and feelings can re-stimulate the nervous system into 'acting out', sometimes called catharsis. Feeling the impulses in the senses and not acting out is what makes this work safer, not so scary and dramatic. In his newest book, <u>In An Unspoken Voice</u>, Dr. Levine relates a case study of a woman who escaped from one of the towers during the horror of 9-11. The woman sought him out after seeing him on TV. He describes sessions with her, what was said, how she reacted. She was able to reclaim her life.

In one of my sessions with Jan, I 'felt' my body tense. It felt hot and surging. Jan encouraged me to let the body feeling(s) flow, and ask what I wanted to do. I said, "I want to scream and kick Billy in the balls. I want to yell at his mother to call the cops and watch them take him away. I want her to take me home to tell Mom what happened." I then followed my body's suggestions and yelled. The experience of thawing felt like surges of vibrations or shudders circulating throughout the body. I took my foot off the brake.

Another invaluable resource is Dr. Alan Wolfell's book, <u>Living in the Shadow of the Ghosts of Grief; Step into the Light</u>. "When you suffer a loss of any kind (like the loss of childhood innocence, my words), you normally and naturally grieve inside. To heal your grief, you must express it. That is,

you must mourn your grief (mourning grief means to outwardly express it, in some way, my words.)

If you don't, you will carry your grief into your future, and it will undermine your happiness for the rest of your life. The good news is that with commitment and the help of a compassionate companion, you can heal your carried grief and go on to live a life of joy."

++++++++++++++++++++

My daughter and I are doing well in Albuquerque. I continue to see my compassionate companion, Jan, less frequently now. I worked as a facilitator for the Children's Grief Center in Albuquerque for three years. Now, I'm writing prose and poetry, loving, forgiving and listening to my body responses.

To know that God is always with us is to cast out all fear—of other people, other religions, others who look and act differently, and those who hurt us, whom we can't forgive.

God is continually telling us, I am the Center of your life; don't be distracted by all that is going on about you; don't be swayed by the emotions of the crowd, the media, the politicians, the world situation; hold fast to Me; stay with Me in the Center, know that I am with you always.

It is our journey to acknowledge fears, prejudices, unforgiveness, feelings of unworthiness, self-condemnation, etc. It takes much inner work. It is not easy. Living a whole life is about knowing that our lives are like spirals, the DNA spiral; it's not sequential. It spirals in and out. Our lives are like the child's toy, the Slinky, we go round and round for awhile, then we go to the next round, never all the way back down.

And the journey continues. My eyes are opened to new awarenesses of God's Grace and the bed-rock knowledge that we are all Loved and cherished. We are here to be God's co-creators of Love and forgiveness, and in tune with our own body awareness and how God interacts with us. Sometimes we have to be in the belly of the whale, so to speak, to know Whose we are and what we're about, never as easy journey, for sure. And new adventures await us each day, as we listen to God's sure guidance.

My ex-husband, Ron, died in December 2012. Diane and I went to see him before he died. At one point I realized that I still loved him and I was able to tell him that I still loved the soul that I married. He said, "Me, too." – a healing experience and closure for me.

Harold Kushner writes in the preface to Victor Frankl's, <u>Man's Search for Meaning</u>: "Frankl saw three possible sources for meaning: in work (doing something significant), in love (caring for another person), and in courage during difficult times. " Ron was not able to be a faithful husband, but, in retrospect, I believe that the meaning of his life was fulfilled by the courage he exhibited in dealing with blindness at the age of 19, and all his later accomplishments.

And last, but not least, is a poem about my Mother and Father, those primary people. I finally knew them, forgave them for perceived wrongs, and carry them in my heart.

ANCIENT DNA

At seven-years old, an alien step-child,
the needle that pierced her last nerve. She
submerged him in caustic waters of
frustration. He rose, like a Phoenix,
burying cries of loneliness and grief deep in his soul,
fleeing to the wilderness.

Cast adrift at three-years old, she, too,
an alien shunted to foreign
places, never at home, only red rose
s to comfort her grief.
The cry of wildness and adventure called.

Their wounded souls merged in
New Mexico in 1929.   The devastated heritage
buried in bone-marrow. Two children arrived,
a boy in 1934 and a girl in 1936. The inherited DNA
and fractured cells totally transferred.

Longing for love, cries of loneliness and anger,
created a vacuum of poverty for the girl, juicy
and ripe for a predator. Seductive violation
shattered boundaries of childhood innocence.
plunging her into altered realities of
fetid feelings and thoughts.

Eons of slogging in the swamp, she finally reached
the edge of solid ground, greeted by music,
Light and laughter, the sound of Love.

Light blooms in her, now the witness, not the actor.
The DNA changed. Fresh breezes blow.

# # #